MY ACCIDENTAL DISCOVERY OF LORD SHIVA

NISHCHAL PADHYA

ISBN 979-8-89363-911-7

Why write a book on Discovery of Lord Shiva, when at the first place, it is just an accidental discovery of Lord Shiva?

This is a very logical question to the mind of any person or the reader of the book, after all, the author is not a religious expert on Hinduism or an accomplished historian or any research scholar.

However, it would be interesting to know how any person, particularly a foreigner not living in India, or who doesn't know much about our Gods and Hinduism, if has any question about Lord Shiva or wants to know about him, where and how he would find out or know and where from? It's obvious, ask Google….

So, let's ask Google and see what it has to say about Lord Shiva? Type "Lord Shiva" in the Google search box and at the first Page Wikipedia says something like this as below:

"Shiva (/ˈʃɪvə/; Sanskrit: शिव, lit. 'The Auspicious One', IAST: Śiva [ɕɪʋɐ]), also known as Mahadeva (/məˈhɑːˈdeɪvə/; Sanskrit: महादेव:, lit. 'The Great God', IAST: Mahādevaḥ, [mɐɦaːdeːʋɐh])[9][10][11] is one of the principal deities of Hinduism.[12] He is the Supreme Being in Shaivism, one of the major traditions within Hinduism.[13]

Shiva is known as The Destroyer within the Trimurti, the Hindu trinity which also includes Brahma and Vishnu.[2][14] In the Shaivite tradition, Shiva is the Supreme Lord who creates, protects and transforms the universe.[9][10][11] In the goddess-oriented Shakta tradition, the Supreme Goddess (Devi) is regarded as the energy and creative power (Shakti) and the equal complementary partner of Shiva.[15][16]

Shiva is one of the five equivalent deities in Panchayatana puja of the Smarta tradition of Hinduism.[17]

Shiva has many aspects, benevolent as well as fearsome. In benevolent aspects, he is depicted as an omniscient Yogi who lives an ascetic life on Mount Kailash[2] as well as a householder with his wife Parvati and his two children, Ganesha and Kartikeya. In his fierce aspects, he is often depicted slaying demons. Shiva is also known as Adiyogi (the first Yogi), regarded as the patron god of yoga, meditation and the arts.[18] The iconographical attributes of Shiva are the serpent king Vasuki around his neck, the adorning crescent moon, the holy river Ganga flowing from his matted hair, the third eye on his forehead (the eye that turns everything in front of it into ashes when opened), the trishula or trident as his weapon, and the damaru. He is usually worshipped in the aniconic form of lingam.[3]

Shiva has pre-Vedic roots,[19] and the figure of Shiva evolved as an amalgamation of various older non-Vedic and Vedic deities, including the Rigvedic storm god Rudra who may also have non-Vedic origins,[20] into a single major deity.[21] Shiva is a pan-Hindu deity, revered widely by Hindus in India, Nepal, Bangladesh, Sri Lanka and Indonesia (especially in Java and Bali)."

It can be thus seen that Wikipedia explains Lord Shiva as Supreme Being and that he lived at Mount Kailash in the Himalayas with his wife Parvati and sons Karthik & Ganesha. And so on, a general explanation with focus on Lord Shiva as an important deity in Hinduism.

Going further, amongst the various search results, it directs one to the website of Lotus Sculpture, the website carries a Picture explaining Lord Shiva with his appearance and accessories as below:

Shiva
The Destroyer

Shiva is the most popular of all Hindu deities. He is worshiped throughout the Indian subcontinent and greater southeast Asia. He is revered as the lord who is responsible for maintaining the cycle of existence; including its beginning and conclusion.

TRIDENT (TRISHULA)
The Trishula represents Shiva's three aspects of "creator, preserver and destroyer," or alternatively, it represents the equilibrium of three Gunas, "sattva, rajas and tamas"

COBRA (VASUKI)
Symbolically, the snake represents passion and desires. By wearing the snake around his neck, Shiva conveys to all of his devotees that he has overcome his earthly desires

THE BULL (NANDI)
Nandi is the symbol of dharma. When you are righteous and truthful, the infinite, innocent consciousness is with you

LINGAM
This is a phallic statue. The Lingam represents the raw power of Shiva and his masculinity. Hindus believe that it represents the seed of the universe, demonstrating Shiva's quality of creation

RIVER GANGA
The The Ganga River is flowing from Lord Shiva's divine head. The meaning of Ganga is knowledge. Threfore, ultimate knowledge is flowing from Lord Shiva

THIRD EYE
Shiva's third eye signifies the destruction of the world of Maya. It is an eye of wisdom, which provides us the faculty to distinguish what is right and what is wrong

TIGER SKIN
Lord Shiva wears a tiger skin which symbolises the victory of the divine force over animal instincts

ROSARY BEADS
Shiva carries a string of rosary beads in his right hand, typically made of Rudraksha. This symbolises grace, mendicant life, and meditation

"Om Namah Shivaya"
"O salutations to the auspicious one!"
Chanting this mantra calms the mind and brings spiritual insight and knowledge

WHAT IS THE TRIMURTI?
The Trimūrti is the triple deity of supreme divinity in Hinduism in which the cosmic functions of creation, maintenance, and destruction are personified as a triad of deities. Typically, Brahma the creator, Vishnu the preserver, and Shiva the destroyer, though individual denominations may vary from that particular line-up

PLACEMENT
It is most ideal to place lord Shiva &/or his Lingam in the northeastern most part of the mandir or whatever space chosen; as is tradition with most murtis. Another reason for this is that it is said lord Shiva & goddess Parvati reside on mount Kailash and that the symbolic placing of Shiva, Ganesh, & Parvati murtis in northeastern corners is done in homage to this myth

Thus, it can be seen that the symbolic explanation of Lord Shiva is focused only on the spiritual philosophy and none of the explanation is leading to any proper logical understanding.

Therefore, after understanding about Lord Shiva, not relying upon any written or knowledge-based material from any religious books, domain experts, although just by accident, in this book, I have tried to bring about a logical explanation about the Lord Shiva.

Every aspect about the Lord Shiva explained in this book would be found thought provoking and absolutely leading to a most logical understanding. If one visits ancient temples and observes the carvings and various designs chiselled on the stones, it can be clearly seen that the ancient Hindus have depicted the understanding of life, yoga, medicine, science & technology and spiritual wisdom through meditation, almost everything in Hinduism can be related to science & technology and general knowledge, Hinduism is way of living life on this earth.

Stories and dramatics have always kept most of the people amused and entertained, and therefore, the story books, plays, cinema & general entertainment has always thrived and therefore, has become a means of communication with masses, an act of play, or drama or pictures always become a very important and easy tool to put across a message or share knowledge and therefore, the ancient Hindus also used it extensively to communicate with masses, and therefore, in order to explain the earth and the concepts of living on it, an imaginative character of Lord Shiva was carved out and co related with the aspects of living life on earth, and to understand the earth itself. May be, because the learning materials and basic education with respect to technical studies were not accessible to public in large,

PANCHAVARNASVAMY TEMPLE

the concepts of the science of the world and scientific principles of living on this earth were not possible to be communicated to masses, to ensure that by and large the earth and the main concepts of living on this earth are understood and followed by masses, it may have been found inevitable to introduce Lord Shiva as God and super power, doing anything wrong against the God was propagated as sinful activity and therefore, masses would by and large refrain from doing such things which would not be appreciated by the God Lord Shiva thus meeting the real objectives of ancient Hindus of understanding our earth and living on it.

Most of the ancient Hindu temples in India and other countries carry so many artistic representations of life on earth and also scientific concepts, if one observes such carvings on ancient temples carefully, the same can be co-related to living life on this earth and the science of this world, there aren't many ancient temples left now, the Moghul invaders destroyed so many such temples which were standing technical evidence to prove that the Hindu religion is purely based upon the science of this world and as such a way of living life.

Well, only fools challenge the science of this world, and therefore, if any person be it an Atheist, Christian, Muslim, Jew, or any other religion, if he /she believes in the science of this world and the concepts of living on earth, first he / she is a Hindu and then any other religion, this is quite obvious, as none of the other religion seem to have concepts of living life on scientific principles except the Hindu religion.

As the Science of this world was always there and shall continue to remain, so would the Hindu religion, it was always there and it shall continue to remain, it's Sanatan (eternal).

TAXI

Therefore, For Hindus, living life on earth with all others is based upon the understanding of "Vasudhaiva Kutumbakam" world is one family. Hinduism doesn't have any confined borders; it's there everywhere in the world.

As my understanding of the concepts of Lord Shiva completely changed due to my accidental understanding of Lord Shiva, I thought that I should publish a small book on this subject "My Accidental Discovery of Lord Shiva". Below narrated are the sequences and thoughts which developed into My Accidental Discovery of Lord Shiva.

I was attending my Japanese agent who was on a business trip to Mumbai, I asked him how his day he explored Mumbai on his own was? He said he had some fantastic road side food with his taxi driver, vegetable burger (Vada Pav) six of them in all as he liked it very much and that he spent large part of the day exploring the south Mumbai city and looking out to buy an artefact showing the picture of an extremely handsome Indian Rock Star which he saw on the dashboard of the local taxi he had hired to get a drop to south Mumbai but could not find the kind he saw on the dashboard of the taxi.

He was so much impressed by the picture of the Indian Rockstar that he saw in the taxi that he just wanted me to buy one for him, I could not understand which Indian Rockstar picture he might have seen on the dashboard of the taxi?

I asked him to describe the Indian Rockstar he was refereeing, to which he went on something like this:

"The guy is well built, looks very handsome, has long hair tied up on head, has a very pleasing face, the guy has a very different sense of fashion and

wears some kind of different fashion accessories all over his body, has a snake as his necklace, wears a kind of shawl made out of leopard skin, some kind of tattoo on the forehead and holds a trident, who is he? And what is his name? I am simply impressed with this guy & want to carry this picture with LED lamps flashing around the same like I saw in the Taxi".

I realized that he had seen the picture of Lord Shiva and I told him the same with a small laugh as I found his description of Lord Shiva being an Indian Rockstar very amusing.

He asked me who is this, Lord Shiva? What is the significance of him being depicted like this and does it mean anything in specific or does it have any special meaning in Hinduism?

I was a bit puzzled with so many questions on Lord Shiva? As a Hindu Brahmin all that I knew about Lord Shiva was that he is our Ishta Dev (main god preached by most of the Brahmins), I had never read much on Hindu mythology and did not quite have much of knowledge on Lord Shiva except that what is told to most of the Hindu children by parents & grandparents during routine prayers or as bed time stories and during religious festivals.

Therefore, I was not quite able to comprehend a suitable instant answer in reply to all his questions on Lord Shiva and I was also wondering if he would really understand the way we Hindus actually consider Lord Shiva.

Well, now I had to explain my guest from Japan who is this, Lord Shiva? I showed him some more pictures of Lord Shiva then something came to my mind and I

thought there cannot be anything better than it explaining Lord Shiva to the mind of a Japanese person who thinks Lord Shiva to be an Indian Rockstar.

I went ahead to explain Lord Shiva something like this:

"Lord Shiva is one of the most popular & very important God amongst millions of other Gods for Hindus all over the world. Lord Shiva is considered to be the God of both creation and destruction; Shiva is also represented by the Lingam which depicts the confluence of the masculine & feminine energies (also addressed as Shakti / Power) due to which the process of initiation of new life continues on this earth. It is with this power that the humans & animals come into existence on this earth in the form of new life on the earth".

This much itself was kind of a good start, my guest got quite interested, so I went on:

"This sign of lingam also indicates that the power of Lingam alone is the right way of loving relationship between a couple leading to continued creation of new life on earth, the mankind should thus remember that becoming a gay or lesbians and proliferation of the same kind of relationship could be one of the reasons leading to the path of end of this world for which we human beings alone would be responsible.

"Generally, the body of Lord Shiva is largely shown in blue colour which could be compared to the huge ocean and sea water on the earth, we all know that 70% of the earth is water, scanty clothes in the form of skin of the leopard or a tiger worn by Lord Shiva could be compared to the land mass of our earth which is just 30%, the fountain of water coming from the head of the Lord Shiva is snow covered mountains and the long hair covering the same provide much needed

insulation for holding & controlling the rapid melting of snow into water thus ensuring two things, one that all the living beings humans and animals including flora and fauna on earth get steady pure source of drinking water and two, the world does not get engulfed into water marking the end of the world which also means destructions, I think ancient Hindus knew about the concept of Global Warming millions of years much ahead of all of us".

By now I was getting a feeling that actually I am re-discovering Lord Shiva myself, so I went ahead and developed some more meaningful thoughts like this:

"Hindus believe that the balance of the earth is on the head of the snake (the Shesh Nag) and therefore, in case the snake shakes his head there would be massive earth quakes and tsunamis and the world could come to an end, this also indicates that since snakes live in burrowed holes in the earth, the mankind before undertaking massive development of land & mining should be careful as by doing so unreasonably or excessively could disturb the land table which could in turn disturb the snake of Lord Shiva and this could trigger massive earth quakes and tsunamis which could lead to destructions of the world.

The trident (the Trishul) pointing to the sky could be compared to one, the protective Ozone layer which protects the life on earth from harsh and harmful IR & UV rays from the sun, two, the environmental cover of the earth that breaks the falling meteors into dust, three, ensuring movement of earth on its course in the orbit thus giving the protection to life from celestial catastrophes, the musical drum (the Dumroo) indicates the noise of the clouds in the skies amongst which the earth is located.

Now, if we will not take care of pollution and harmful chemicals, the ozone layer could get depleted and the life on earth could get exposed to harmful IR & UV rays of the sun and spoil our environment & weather thus leading to destruction of the earth.

The Rudraksh necklace, bracelet and pendent reminds about gravitational power of the earth, all of us on this earth as Rudrakshas are moving on this earth, tied around it and cannot drift away into the space, the tying around the Lord Shiva is the gravitational power of the earth.

Lord Shiva due to his immense anger in case opens his third eye, the world would be burnt into ashes instantly, actually this third eye depicts the potential of nuclear energy, by this feature of third eye, Lord Shiva indicates to the mankind that in case we misuse this energy by proliferating nuclear weapons our world would come to an end and thus the sign of destruction.

Therefore, Lord Shiva is actually nothing but our Earth; it is only here that life cycle exists due to its unique features like water, oxygen and therefore Lord Shiva is also known as creator and destroyer.

All pictures of Lord Shiva are always shown wearing a moon shaped broach on the head of Lord Shiva, the fact that Lord Shiva wears the moon on his head actually proves that he is himself nothing but our earth as the moon being satellite of earth always revolves around earth."

Listening to my explanation of Lord Shiva meaning nothing but to be but our earth, my guest from Japan was extremely impressed, I arranged the picture of Lord Shiva which he gladly accepted and took away with him to Japan.

I thought I just re-discovered Lord Shiva completely my way based upon my own philosophy, before sharing these thoughts with my friends and family, I again gave it a thought and it came to my mind that the Hindu mythology considers Lord Ganesha to be the son of Lord Shiva and this fact firmed up my belief much stronger, Lord Ganesh is half human and half animal and therefore, it makes me think that since the earth is mainly inhabited by Humans and animals both, and since Lord Shiva is considered as father, then he is nothing but our earth. Actually, Lord Ganesha was designed to explain the masses that they are not the only privileged ones to enjoy living life on earth and claiming its right over the resources of this earth all alone, the animals shall have equal rights over the resources of the earth, this fact of living life on earth had to be communicated properly to the masses, and therefore, like how Lord Shiva was designed to explain the features of our Earth and living life on it, the ancient Hindus designed Lord Ganesha half human and half animal to strongly drive the point that animals shall continue to have their rights over the earth much same like we human beings. So therefore, as sons of Lord Shiva, the Humans and Animals both shall be equal before the Lord Shiva and so the equal rights over the Lord Shiva, which essentially means, equal rights over the earth on which both humans and animals shall have to exist and live life.

I went ahead and then shared my views on this new discovery of Lord Shiva to be nothing but our Earth with my family and friends, some of them were pleasantly surprised and amused with my new understanding of Lord Shiva, my wife encouraged

me to write on these thoughts and share it with all and therefore this book. In my understanding our Hindu religion is completely based upon scientific principle and therefore, perhaps is the most practical religion based on facts and reality of day to day living of humans, animals and behaviour of the nature on our earth (Lord Shiva).

Actually, this real understanding of Lord Shiva to be our earth and concepts of living on it certainly leads to the understanding that "Hinduism" is indeed the way of living life on earth, as time passed since the conceptualisation of Lord Shiva to be our earth and concepts of living on it, this real understanding remained lost somewhere and the Lord Shiva being a God and super power continued as the understanding of masses including almost everyone.

I feel that the teachings and learnings of our Rishimunies (Hindu Scientists) have been accidentally understood by me and now **I feel that Lord Shiva is our very Earth**. The Rishimunies probably knew the science of this world millions of years back, but since may be the language, knowledge and understanding of the masses in general was not developed enough to understand the science of this world and the lifecycle itself, the concept of Lord Shiva would have been created by imagination for the ease of understanding of our earth and living on it. Perhaps, over the millions of years we people still could not understand that Lord Shiva is actually our Earth, All the humans living on this earth shall necessarily have to understand the earth & concepts of living on it, and therefore, Lord Shiva would have to be understood on the basis of this accidental discovery of Lord Shiva, thus Lord Shiva belongs to all irrespective of religion, caste, creed, colour, region, country and for all of us, **its Lord Shiva = Our Earth & Concepts of living on it!**

[Disclaimer: These are my very own personal thoughts based upon my access to and extent of the knowledge of the subject, logical & philosophical understanding of Lord Shiva, and my intentions are not to harm religious feelings or believes of any other person/s]

Any suggestions, comments and thoughts are welcome to nishchal.padhya@gmail.com

Nishchal Padhya

Har Har Mahadev.